Start Maths
FIRST STEPS

Numbers

Ann Montague-Smith

QED Publishing

First published in the UK in 2004 by
QED Publishing
A Quarto Group Company
226 City Road
London, EC1V 2TT

www.qed-publishing.co.uk

A Catalogue record for this book is available from the British Library.

ISBN 978 1 84835 132 5

Written by Ann Montague-Smith
Designed and edited by The Complete Works
Illustrated by Jenny Tulip
Photography by Steve Lumb and Michael Wicks

Creative Director Louise Morley
Editorial Manager Jean Coppendale

Printed and bound in China

With thanks to: ELC

4 - 1 = 3

Contents

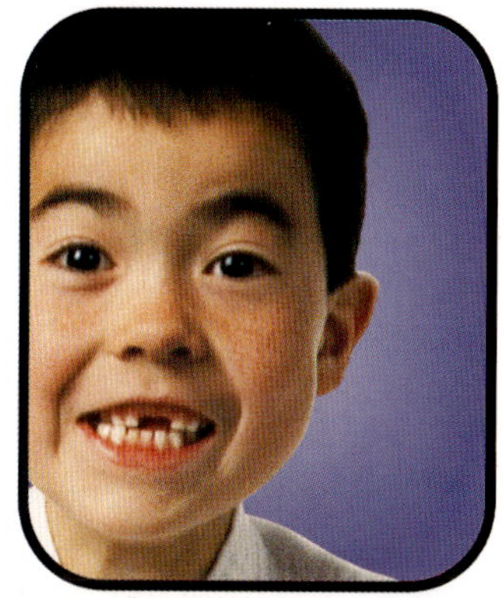

How many are there?

There were 3 dogs in a basket. 1 dog fell out. How many dogs are in the basket now?

There were 2 dogs in a basket. 1 dog fell out. How many dogs are in the basket now?

Use your fingers. Show how many dogs are left in the basket each time.

There was 1 dog in the basket. He fell out. How many dogs are in the basket now?

Challenge

You will need a cup, 3 bricks and a friend. Hide some of the bricks under the cup and show what is left. Can your friend say how many bricks are under the cup?
Now swap over.

Who has 4?

Look carefully at the pictures.
Find the girls holding up 4 fingers.

Look at each picture.
How many more fingers will make 5?

Challenge

You will need a friend and 5 counters. Both put your hands behind your back. Then both hold up one hand and show some fingers. Whoever shows more fingers can take a counter. The winner is the one who has more counters when all the counters are gone.

Make it 1 more

Count the elephants.

How many would there be if there were 1 more?

Count each set of animals.

Say how many there would be if there were 1 more.

4 - 1 = 3

Challenge

Draw a set of 3 cats.
How many would there
be if you drew 1 more cat?
Draw the cat to check.
Try this for 4 dogs.
How about 5 rabbits?

Say 1 fewer

Count how many. Say how many.

Now say how many if there were 1 fewer.

What if there were 1 more?

How many then?

4 - 1 = 3

Challenge

Lay a table for 3 people with knives and forks.
How many knives and how many forks did you need?
What if 1 person did not come?
How many of each would you need then?

Make it 4

Count how many drums there are.
How many more do you need to make 4?

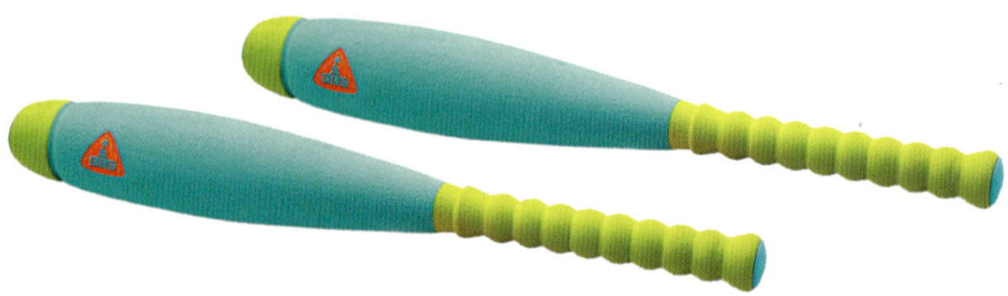

Count each of the other sets.
How many more do you need to make 4?

4 - 1 = 3

Challenge

Take turns to do this with a friend. You will need 5 bricks. One of you puts some bricks in a line. The other says how many more bricks are needed to make 5.

Total 2 sets

Count 1 set of fruit. How many is that?

Now count the other set of fruit. How many is that?

Now count all the fruits. How many is that altogether?

Which plates have 5 fruits on them?

Challenge

Do this with a friend.
Get 8 counters.
Both of you take some counters. Count how many you have each.
Now count all of these counters to find out how many you have altogether.
Do this 3 more times.

Total 3 sets

Count the dogs, count the cats and count the rabbits in each set. Now count all the animals in each set. How many are there altogether?

Which sets have 4 animals?

4 - 1 = 3

Challenge

Count out 6 counters and divide them onto two place mats. How many counters altogether on the mats?

Make totals

Choose a set of toys. Count the toys. Do this again.
Now count and say how many toys there are altogether.
Can you find 2 sets which total 3?
Now see if you can find 2 sets which total 4.

Can you find 3 sets which will total 4?
Can you do this in 2 different ways?

4 - 1 = 3

Challenge

Find 2 sets of toys which total 6.

Can you find 3 different ways to do this?

Now can you find 2 sets which total 7?

Solve a problem

Find 2 sets of sweets which total 5.

How many different ways can you find to do this?

Can you find 3 sets of sweets which total 5?

How many different ways can you find to do this?

4 - 1 = 3

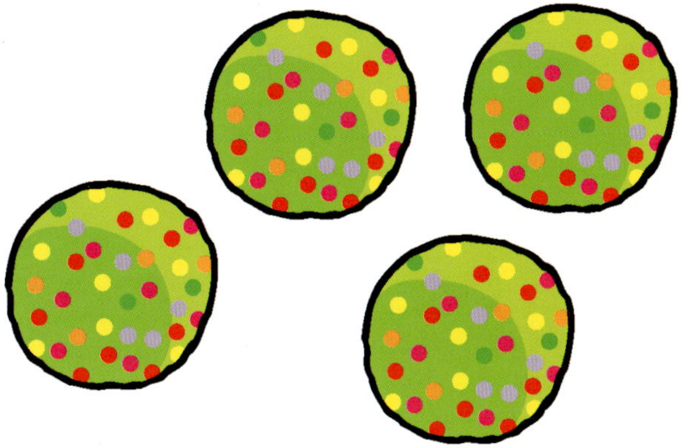

Challenge

Find 3 sets of sweets which total 6.
Now can you make a total of 7?
What about a total of 8?

Supporting notes for adults

How many are there? – pages 4-5

This activity introduces the idea of zero. Discuss how, when all the dogs have fallen out of the basket, there are none left. If children are unsure about this, ask them to show you 3 fingers, then 2, 1, and none.

Who has 4? – pages 6-7

Encourage the children to count how many fingers are showing for each child on the page. If they are unsure, ask them to hold up the same number of fingers, then to count their own fingers.

Make it 1 more – pages 8-9

If children are unsure about 1 more, ask them to count the set, for example 3 animals. Now ask them to say the counting numbers 1, 2, 3, 4, so that they count 1 more than 3.

Say 1 fewer – pages 10-11

Where there is 1 item in the set, 1 fewer will be zero, or nothing. If children are unsure about this, then count back from 5: 5, 4, 3, 2, 1, 0. Do this several times.

Make it 4 – pages 12-13

Encourage the children to count on from how many there are in each set until they reach 4. They can keep count on their fingers. For example, if there are 2 things, then they count 3, 4, at the same time putting up 1 finger for each number they say: 2 fingers.

Total 2 sets – pages 14-15

Encourage the children to count 1 set of fruit, then the other. Now ask them to count all the fruit on the plate so that they can say the total. You may like the children to say the number sentence for this. For example: 1 apple and 2 oranges. That is 3 pieces of fruit altogether.

Total 3 sets – pages 16-17

Encourage the children to count each set, then to count them all. Say, 'How many did you count? What was the last number you said? So how many animals are there altogether?'

Make totals – pages 18-19

Begin by asking the children to count each set and to say how many there are. Now invite them to count a set, then count on for another set to make a total. It is possible to make totals of up to 8 by combining 2 sets. This will extend the activity for the more able children.

Solve a problem – pages 20-21

If children find this difficult, model the problem using counters or bricks. The children can put out counters to match the number of sweets in each set, then find which will combine to make 5.

Suggestions for using this book

Children will enjoy looking through the book and talking about the colourful pictures. Sit somewhere comfortable together. Please read the instructions to the children, then encourage them to take part in the activity and check whether or not they have understood what to do.

Help them to count how many by asking them to touch each picture, then say the number together. Ask questions such as, 'What was the last number you said? So, how many … are there?' This will help the children to recognize that when counting, the last number word that they say will tell them how many there are altogether.

If they are unsure about the concept of 1 more and 1 fewer, suggest that they use their fingers, and show you, say, 4 fingers. Now say, 'How could you show me 1 fewer?' Encourage them to put one finger down, and to show you 3 fingers, for example. Now say, 'How many are there now?' This can be repeated for 1 more.

Where children are asked to total two sets, encourage them to count each set separately, then to count all of them together. So, for 3 birds and 2 birds they would count 1, 2, 3. 1, 2. 1, 2, 3, 4, 5. Now say a number sentence together such as '2 and 3 makes 5.' Totalling is extended to totalling 3 sets and this can be tackled in the same way.

Page 20 contains some simple problems for the children to solve. Encourage them to find one way to do this, then to look for other ways. If you are working with a group of children, they can share their responses and explain why their solution works to the other children.